This book belongs to:

____

Made in the USA
Las Vegas, NV
25 February 2022

44603345R10066